Reading & Writing

A Gift from the Gods

Reading & Writing

A Gift from the Gods

mc **Marshall Cavendish**
Benchmark
New York

This edition first published in 2009 in North America by Marshall Cavendish Benchmark.

Marshall Cavendish Benchmark
99 White Plains Road
Tarrytown, NY 10591
www.marshallcavendish.us

Library of Congress Cataloging-in-Publication Data

Rossi, Renzo, 1940–
  A gift from the gods / by Renzo Rossi.
    p. cm. — (Reading and writing)
  ISBN 978-0-7614-4318-6
  1. Writing—History—Juvenile literature. I. Title.
  P211.R669 2009
  411.09—dc22
                              2008032288

Text: Renzo Rossi
Editing: Cristiana Leoni
Translation: Erika Pauli
Design and layout: Luigi Ieracitano
Illustrations: Alessandro Baldanzi, Lorenzo Cecchi, Sauro Giampaia, Luigi Ieracitano

Photographs: Scala Archives pp. 11, 28

Printed in Malaysia
1 3 5 6 4 2

Contents

A Secret Writing

The signs with which the ancient Egyptians wrote are called hieroglyphs, which means "incised sacred words." They look like some kind of secret, mysterious writing, invented in the most remote of times. The earliest examples known can be dated to even before the pharaoh Narmer united Egypt, over 5,000 years ago. Yet these signs are no longer mysterious and scholars have been able to read them for over a hundred years.

Above: All hieroglyphs must be similar in size, whether they represent a tiny beetle or an enormous hippo.

Hieroglyphs represent real things: objects, plants, animals, human figures, parts of the body, and so on—things everyone can recognize—and every sign stands for what it represents. Yet hieroglyphic signs also indicate the sounds of these words. By grouping together several signs a person can write names or form words that cannot be shown directly—almost a game, like a rebus where the spoken word for a pictured object resembles the spoken word (or syllable of a word) that is difficult to portray as a glyph.

Below: These hieroglyphs were inscribed on a stone vase during the 3rd millennium BCE. They are the names of pharaohs who reigned during that time.

Below: Fish (NAR) + chisel (MER) = Narmer. Narmer is the earliest known king of Egypt (c. 3000 BCE).

Right: A wooden sarcophagus is covered with hieroglyphs made of brightly colored glass. Since many signs are repeated more than once, we know that in this case they stand for sounds or syllables rather than words.

Right: This palette illustrates the feats of the pharaoh Narmer, whose name is carved below the top panel. The hieroglyph is made of two symbols that, when read together, mean "Narmer."

How Hieroglyphs Work

When hieroglyphs were used to transcribe syllables or sounds, they indicated only the consonants; Egyptian writing didn't take the vowels into account. Therefore, the same sign can have more than one meaning.

In order to avoid confusion, another category of signs—called determinatives—was added. Determinatives are not pronounced but, when associated with a glyph, indicate its meaning.

For example, all the words that indicate movement are followed by a drawing of two legs shown walking.

Below: In Egyptian writing, alphabet glyphs express the sound of one letter, biliteral glyphs express the sound of two letters, and triliteral glyphs express the sound of three letters. Vowels have been added to the words below the glyphs to make them easier to pronounce.

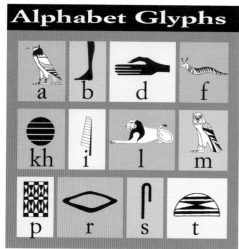

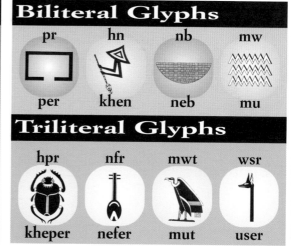

This painted stone head is a bust of the princess Nofret, who lived around 2700 BCE. Her name is written by combining five glyphs. The glyph on the right is pronounced NFR, but it has been reinforced by the glyphs *viper* (F), *mouth* (R), and *bread* (T). The crouching female figure is the determinative for female names. It is not pronounced.

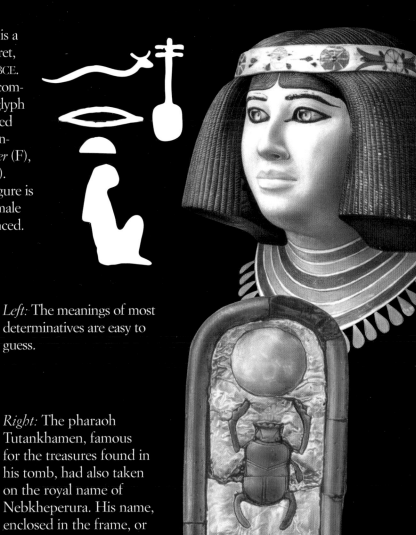

man

king

movement

woman or queen

Left: The meanings of most determinatives are easy to guess.

Right: The pharaoh Tutankhamen, famous for the treasures found in his tomb, had also taken on the royal name of Nebkheperura. His name, enclosed in the frame, or *cartouche* (*right*), is written with four glyphs. NEB (basket) + KHEPER (scarab beetle) + RA (sun). The fourth sign, the three sticks, represents the sound PRU. This sign reinforces the PR in KHEPER and adds a U-sound before RA.

Everyday Writing

Writing a text in detailed and minute hieroglyphs takes a lot of time. This complex script was, therefore, used only for official occasions; drawn in color on the walls of the tombs; or chiseled onto monuments, statues, or temples.

Over time the pictorial sign was gradually simplified for everyday use. This cursive writing—called hieratic, or sacred—was used mostly by the priests. Later, the hieratic script was further simplified to make an even quicker and more concise script known as demotic, which means "the people's writing."

Opposite: The *Book of the Dead* was written on papyrus in the 14th century BCE. It contains formulas written in hieroglyphics and hieratic script to help the deceased in their journeys to the other world.

Below: The evolution from hieroglyphs to hieratic script to demotic is visible with the characters for *writing.*

Hieroglyphic		Hieratic		Demotic	
2800-2900 BCE	2000-1800 BCE	c. 1900 BCE	c. 1300 BCE	c. 200 BCE	c. 100 BCE

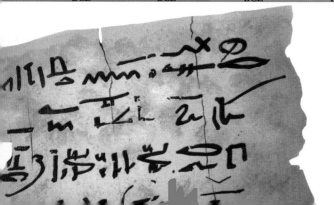

Left: This fragment of papyrus is covered with hieratic script. Writing on papyrus makes it possible to correct errors, which cannot be done when the signs are carved in stone.

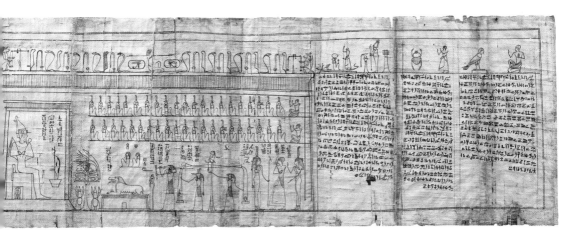

The Egyptians had texts dealing with medicine, mathematics, astronomy, and other subjects, as well as collections of instructions on how to behave in life. The upper class loved books of poetry, short stories, and even adventure stories. The famous *Story of Sinuhe* was often read aloud by scribes during receptions and banquets.

Papyrus

In Egypt, a type of paper is made from the papyrus plant that grows along the Nile River.

To prepare this paper, a craftsperson uses a sharp knife to remove the outer part of the plant from the papyrus stalk. Then the fibrous layers inside are cut into thin, narrow strips. These strips are set one next to another, overlapping at the edges, to form a continuous sheet. This sheet is then crossed at right angles with another layer of strips.

It is pressed and dried, resulting in a compact, elastic sheet that can be joined end-to-end with other sheets to form a roll that is several yards (meters) long.

Left: The papyrus plant, which grows up to 18 feet (6 m) tall, has a triangular, woody stem.

Opposite: There are several steps to making papyrus paper:
1) Remove the outer layer

2) Cut the inner fiber into thin strips

3) Lay down the strips, press them together, and allow the sheet to dry

4) The finished product measures no more than 20 x 16 inches (50 x 40 cm)

Right: A tomb painting from 1400 BCE depicts a laborer carrying a load of papyrus.

Opposite, below: A carving shows two workers pressing a stack of papyrus sheets.

1

2

3

4

back

writing side

The Power of Writing

As we have seen, Egyptian writing is very complex and difficult. Therefore, only a few people could learn it. Reading and writing became a prestigious profession—that of the scribe.

The best scribes were employed by the state administration or in the temples where goods were collected. Scribes went into the fields to take measurements or count the livestock and the harvest, recorded the wares in storerooms, drew up documents in the archives, calculated the laborers' wages in work yards, and collected taxes.

Above: The hieroglyph for *writing* is a picture of a scribe's instruments: a stylus, jars for the red and black colors, and the water vase. All the items were tied with a cord so a scribe could carry them around his neck.

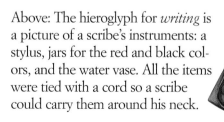

When a scribe was writing on a papyrus scroll he could only use one section at a time. Once he filled the area, he waited for the ink to dry before rolling it up so he could continue writing on a new section. This scribe is holding the stylus; behind his ear are pigment sticks.

Left: Scribes used different kinds of styluses. They carried the styluses in a case and prepared the colors on a palette (*opposite, bottom*).

Opposite, right: These four types of ocher were used by scribes to make the pigments for writing and painting.

In the Far East: China

As in Egypt and Mesopotamia, a unique system of writing was also invented in China around the 3rd millennium BCE. This system of writing used pictographs, or drawings of objects and figures, to represent words. The pictographs were gradually simplified to make writing easier.

Combining the pictographs and giving them symbolic values led to the formation of ideograms, which could express concepts. For example, the sign *woman* under the sign *roof* meant "peace" or "tranquility." The sign *magician* associated with the sign *talking* meant "lying." Thousands of words could be written with this system, but only those who knew the meaning of the ideograms could read them.

Left: Etchings on a tortoise shell dating to 1400 BCE are an early example of Chinese calligraphy.

Opposite and left: The Chinese developed three principal script styles: seal style (*left*) was used for documented records, regular style (*center*) was used for government documents and printed books, and grass style (*right*) simplified regular style by joining words but was not universally readable.

MU

RI

Left: This ideogram is easy to understand. The sign for tree, MU, is written above the sign for sun, RI. This forms the word *darkness*, YAO (the sun covered by the tree).

The character RI, which means "sun," can be doubled to mean "bright" (CHANG). If it is repeated three times it means "blinding" (JING). These are the three degrees of intensity of light.

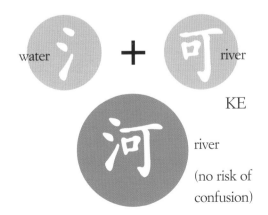

water

+

river

KE

river

(no risk of confusion)

Left: In writing certain words, sometimes the sound, not the figure, is the base. This is the case with the symbol KE, which means "river." So readers don't confuse it with another word that has the same sound, it is preceded by the character for water.

17

The Art of Writing

In China calligraphy has always been considered an art in itself. Writing must be "alive." Every stroke in a piece of calligraphy must have the energy of a living thing, the well-balanced movements of a dance.

In the finest calligraphy every brushstroke presents itself as a powerful unbroken yet harmonious and elegant line. Every stroke seems to be connected to the next by invisible bonds.

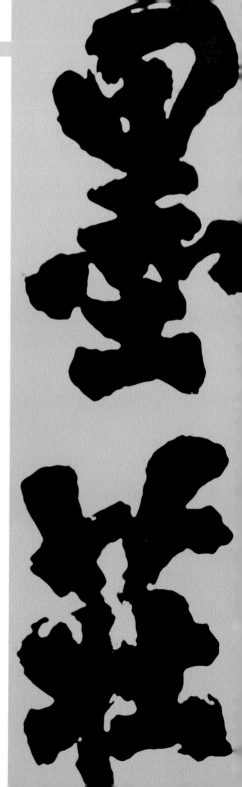

Right: The draw-
ing of a magnolia
branch and
the modern calli-
graphic script are
equally soft and
harmonious.

Opposite: The red
character, which
reads "by order of
the emperor,"
dates to 1100 CE.
The black one is
contemporary
writing.

Below: The eight
fundamental
strokes of Chinese
calligraphy are all
contained in the
written sign
YONG, which
means "eternity."

Chinese Masters of Writing

It is difficult to clearly distinguish between scholars, painters, and calligraphy artists in ancient China. An official with long, hard years of study and difficult exams behind him might be all three. In Europe, only the artists of the Renaissance can be compared. Michelangelo, for example, was a painter, sculptor, architect, and poet.

Below: There are twelve basic strokes in Chinese writing. The green arrows indicate the direction in which the brush should move.

Painting, literature, and calligraphy must, all together, transmit the atmosphere that inspired the work, but at the same time represent reality. The colors and the composition of the calligraphic elements must harmonize with and be a visual equivalent of the text and the feelings aroused.

Right: When writing Chinese calligraphy, the brush is not held the way we hold a pencil or pen. The ink is made by dissolving an ink stick in water.

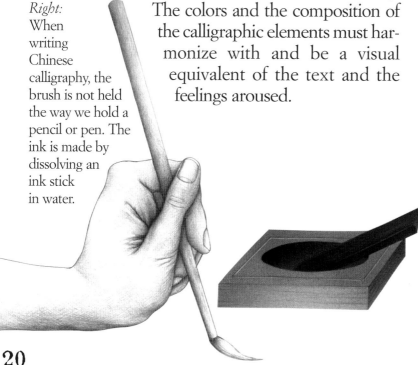

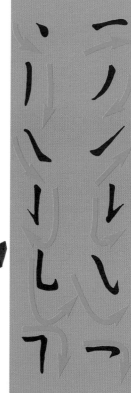

Chinese poets sought inspiration for their works in the harmony of nature. They often brought their writing tools to gardens, riverbanks, or forests to compose their work.

21

From China to Japan

As early as the 4th century CE, the Japanese adopted characters inspired by Chinese writing that were suitable to the Japanese language, which was very different from Chinese. The syllabic writing used today, known as kana, is derived from these signs.

There are two kinds of kana: katakana and hiragana. Katakana is used for foreign words, print advertising, and the like. Hiragana, or "women's hand," is derived from Chinese grass writing and is more elegant and graceful.

Below: The Japanese have two different alphabets: hiragana and katakana. Japanese texts are arranged in columns and are read top to bottom, starting with the column farthest to the right. The first page of a book in Japanese is what would be the last page of a book in English.

	Katakana	Hiragana		Katakana	Hiragana		Katakana	Hiragana		Katakana	Hiragana
i (ha)	イ	い	wa	ワ	わ	w(i)	ヰ	ゐ	sa	サ	さ
ro	ロ	ろ	ka	カ	か	no	ノ	の	ki	キ	き
fa (ho)	ハ	は	jo	ヨ	よ	o	オ	た	ju	ユ	ゆ
ni (he)	ニ	に	ta	タ	た	ku	ク	く	me	メ	め
fo	ホ	ほ	re	レ	れ	ja	ヤ	や	mi	ミ	み
fe (tschi)	ヘ	へ	so	ソ	そ	ma	マ	ま	si (schi)	シ	～
to	ト	と	tu (tsu)	ツ	つ	ke	ケ	け	w(e)	ヱ	ゑ
ti	チ	ち	ne	ネ	ね	fu	フ	ふ	fi (hi)	ヒ	ひ
ri	リ	り	na	ナ	な	ko	コ	こ	mo	モ	も
nu	ヌ	ぬ	ra	ラ	ら	e	エ	ね	se	セ	せ
ru	ル	る	mu	ム	む	te	テ	て	su	ス	す
(w)o	ヲ	を	u	ウ	う	a	ア	あ	n	ン	ん

Above: This red calligraphic symbol is the sign for the word *samurai.*

Right: Calligraphic writing imitates bamboo canes with its elegant lines.

23

Creating a Korean Alphabet

Initially, Chinese script was used in Korea, but in 1446, by decree of King Sejong, scholars and grammarians were called in to compile a new Korean alphabet. The Korean alphabet was created to perfectly adapt to the spoken language. It is based on an extremely simple, linear, and geometric system.

Consonants and vowels are grouped together to form groups of syllables that resemble Chinese characters. These syllables are written in square-shaped units, so Korean writing has a geometric appearance. Like Chinese and Japanese, Korean is written from top to bottom, in columns going from right to left.

Opposite: These ancient Korean printing characters were used before the Korean alphabet was created.

Below: Letters in the Korean alphabet are combined to create the syllables HAN and GUK. *Hanguk* means "Korea." Notice how each syllable is drawn as if inside a square.

Below: Some letters in the Korean alphabet have more than one pronunciation depending on the position within a word.

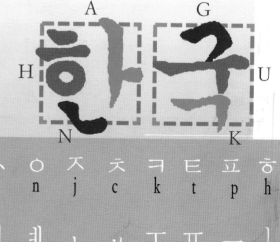

ㄱ	ㄴ	ㄷ	ㄹ	ㅁ	ㅂ	ㅅ	ㅇ	ㅈ	ㅊ	ㅋ	ㅌ	ㅍ	ㅎ
k,g,n	n	t,d,n	l,r	m	p,b,m	s	n	j	c	k	t	p	h

ㅏ	ㅑ	ㅐ	ㅒ	ㅓ	ㅕ	ㅔ	ㅖ	ㅗ	ㅛ	ㅜ	ㅠ	ㅡ	ㅣ
a	ya	ae	yae	ô	yô	e	ye	o	yo	u	yu	û	i

Grammarians gathered together to create a new Korean alphabet, which has 17 consonants and 11 vowels.

In the Land of the Maya

The Maya lived in what is today southern Mexico, Guatemala, Honduras, and El Salvador for more than 2,000 years before the Spanish arrived in 1521. They had an extremely complex system of writing, and the only complete system among the ancient American cultures.

Maya writing consists of a complicated ensemble of signs, or glyphs, carved in stone. A glyph expresses both a concept and a sound. Almost all indicate a single syllable, so that words with two or more syllables are constructed like a rebus, as in Sumerian and Egyptian writing.

Maya writing was also adapted to the Nahuatl language, spoken by the Aztecs, who founded their empire in Mexico around 1300.

Opposite: At the center of this stone disk is a *pelota* (ball) player. The glyphs of the months and numerical signs are in the border.

Opposite, below: In addition to stone, the Maya also wrote and drew on paper made from the wild fig tree. This image of two figures seated by a pot comes from a hand-written book called a codex.

Left: This portrait glyph is of a face with large eyes. It is from a stone relief found in Yaxchilán in Guatemala.

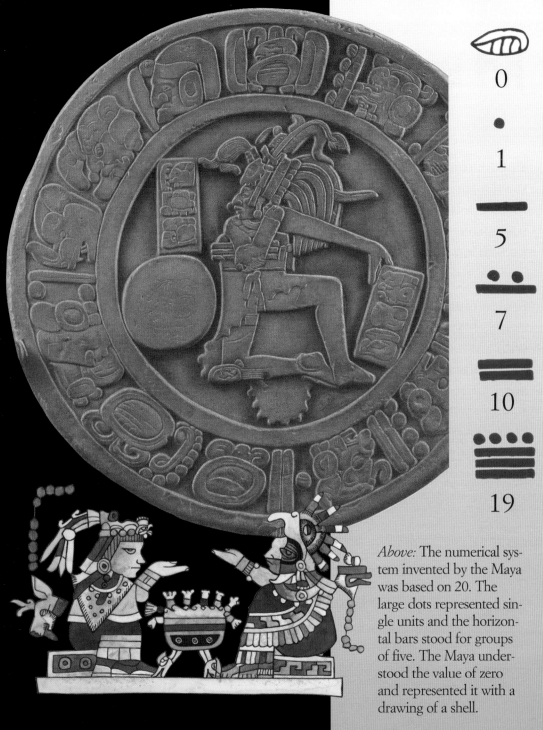

0

1

5

7

10

19

Above: The numerical system invented by the Maya was based on 20. The large dots represented single units and the horizontal bars stood for groups of five. The Maya understood the value of zero and represented it with a drawing of a shell.

All Bark

In addition to sculpting glyphs on temples and palace stones, the Maya and Aztec drew glyphs in bright colors on pottery, tanned animal hides, and long rolls of paper that they made by soaking the bark of the wild fig tree.

They used water-soluble vegetable and mineral colors, ranging from black to gray, blue, green, yellow, ocher, brown, and red. These colors were painted with animal-hair brushes or with pointed instruments of various sizes.

Below: Only four Maya codices have been discovered. The one shown here is a fragment of the *Madrid Codex*, which features painted divinities and glyphs.

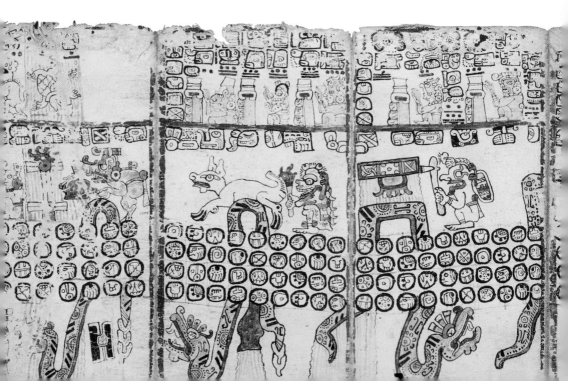

Making Paper

The soaked fibers of the fig tree are pounded on a flat surface and mixed with resin. They are then flattened, smoothed, and dried.

The best quality paper is covered with a layer of lime or plaster to make the figures and signs stand out.

The paper is then folded accordion-style to form a book.

29

Index

Page numbers in **boldface** are illustrations, tables, and charts.